YOU CAN'T BECOME A FOOTBALL OVERNIGHT

A book of "Petersonisms"

Jim Crosby

Seminole Boosters, Inc.
Tallahassee, FL

Writeman Enterprises
3285 Thoreau Avenue
Tallahassee, FL 32311
www.writeman.com

Printed in the United States of America

ISBN: 9780615232850

Photos Courtesy of: Tallahassee Democrat
Florida State University
Vaughn Mancha
The Peterson Family
Associated Press
NoleFan.org
Canopy Road Photography (back cover photo)

Dedication

This book is dedicated to the memory of Robert Urich, one of Coach Pete's boys whose time with us was all too brief. If anyone could "become a football overnight" it would have been this warm-hearted, Emmy-winning, television tough-guy.

Contents

Dedication   3

Contents   5-6

A Proverb   7

Acknowledgements   9-10

Introduction   11-12

The Actor, Robert Urich   13

The President, T.K. Wetherell   14

The Coach, Bobby Bowden   15

Pete's Practices   17-25

The Judge, Kim Hammond   26

Pete at Game Time   27-34

The Magical QB, Gary Huff   35

Pete's Player Descriptions   36-43

The 1st Great QB, Steve Tensi   44

Pete's Philosophy   45-62

The Record Setting QB, Bill Cappleman   63

The Linebacker, Dick Herman   64

Pete's Updates   65-74

Pete's Pearls   75-84

The Namesake, Bill Peterson, Jr.   85

Pete's Accolades   86-88

Pete in the NFL   89-92

Pete's Democracy   93-96

McGrotha's Petersonisms   97-104

The Sportswriter, Bill McGrotha   98

The Wife, Marge Peterson   105

Pete, The Family Man   106-109

Contents

Pete Becomes a Seminole — 110-112

The Athletic Director, Vaughn Mancha — 113

Remembering Pete at the Slipper — 114

Pete's Continuing Success Story — 115-121

Final Thought from Pete — 122

A Fitting Finish — 123

Pete's Posts — 124

FSU's Lasting Tribute to Coach Bill Peterson — 125

A word aptly spoken is like apples of gold in settings of silver.

Proverbs 25:11

Acknowledgements

You Can't Become a Football Overnight is a book that has evolved over quite a few years. Consequently, a lot of folks have contributed to its success.

Foremost among these are the Seminole Boosters, Inc. A big debt of gratitude is owed to President and CEO Andy Miller and Jerry Kutz, Vice President of Marketing and Communications for making sure the book got published. Their dedication to preserving the greatness of the Seminole Past and building a successful future helped this book assume its rightful place in Florida State Football history.

The Peterson Family has been an enthusiastic and generous provider of family history, photos, facts and memorabilia. Special thanks to Marge and Bill Peterson, Jr.

Florida State President T. K. Wetherell shared his special insights into not only Coach Pete's coaching and organizational talents, but his impressive people skills as well.

As always, Coaching Legend Bobby Bowden captured the essence of the project and gave us historic, little-known and funny stories about the Peterson era and his lasting impact on Florida State football.

To all the players who played for Coach Peterson and had their lives shaped by that exposure, I can't thank you enough for your contribution. Those who took time to be interviewed and waited patiently over the years for the book to become a reality are owed a major debt of gratitude. My apologies go out to those who, because of time and space restraints, were not included in the material. That doesn't make your contribution to FSU's storied history any less important or appreciated.

Behind the scenes many people helped. Special thanks are owed to Jim Melton, former Director of the Florida State Alumni Association, for always being willing to help. He is a great sounding board, possesses an abundance of common sense, and is a savvy businessman and friend.

The Florida State Sports Information Department is the best anywhere and my heartfelt thanks go to Rob Wilson, Associate Athletics Director, and Tina Dechaushay, Sports Information Director, for always saying "yes" when asked for help. Special thanks to my friend Dee Frye Davis, FSU's right-hand lady, for sharing her Peterson stories and for her encouragement!

A debt of gratitude goes to Gerald "Perk" Ensley of the Tallahassee Democrat, one of the best writers I know and an unselfish friend who is always willing to help.

Thanks to the many friends and family, especially those at Good Samaritan United Methodist Church, for laughing at the collected quotes and establishing the viability of the book by encouraging me to stick with the project. Foremost among these is The Lovely Susette, my wife, who is the World's Greatest Encourager, a sharp editor, and has a unique sense of what represents quality and what doesn't.

Technically this book worked because of Jerry Kutz's insight as a former editor, Emily Wright's cover design and editing skills with the Florida State Varsity Club, and the quality work of Rose Printing Company in Tallahassee.

We are also grateful to Bob Perrone and Andrew Brady for their great work on NoleFan.org, a very attractive and helpful website.

All of you make a great team. It required each of you to tell the story of one of the All Time Greats in College Football Coaching. Thank you!

Introduction

Standing at a counter in a local convenience store I happened to look out the window. A car came zipping into my line of vision, stopped abruptly in a parking space and the driver quickly emerged. He rushed to the front door and was practically in the store before his car door fully closed behind him. The man strode rapidly to a shelf, picked up a candy bar and started unwrapping and eating it as he walked to the check out station. The candy bar was practically consumed by the time he paid for it.

That was typical of Bill Peterson, Seminole Coaching Legend, a man I had worked with on Florida State University football broadcasts and shared a microphone with on several of my sports talk shows. As I walked up to say hello, I noticed the brand name on the candy wrapper was "Whatchmacallit."

Perhaps that scenario innocently speaks volumes concerning Coach Peterson's life. Always in a hurry to move forward and make things happen, his mind just seemed to race ahead of his tongue. Consequently, the late, great football coach left behind a legacy of delightfully misspoken but insightful sayings called " Petersonisms." They are Bill Peterson's own brand of "whatchamacallits."

The Peterson originals collected in this book are so plentiful they seem to comprise a language of their own. We've labeled it "Petersonese." After all, anyone who could take a football program from practically nowhere to national recognition through creative problem-solving and inventiveness in football strategy, could surely design a language of his own   even if most of it was inadvertent.

Sometimes people said Coach Pete deliberately mixed-up his words to "put-on" his audience, but most of it was the unintentional result of a man in a hurry to make things better.

What follows is the best of the beloved Coach's planned and unplanned statements along with a look at some of the folks who played a prominent role in the life of Bill Peterson — college and pro football coach, husband, father, and friend.

- Jim

Spencer's Favorite
"YOU CAN'T BECOME A FOOTBALL OVERNIGHT... YOU'VE GOT TO WORK AT IT."

At football practice, Bill Peterson often reminded his team of just how much hard work is required to become a champion. This saying was always a favorite of actor Robert Urich, who played center for Coach Peterson before an injury in a memorable game ended his playing career and gave him headaches the rest of his life. The silver lining for Urich was that he became an actor. He was best known for his television role in *Spencer for Hire*. Urich became highly successful because he knew "he couldn't become an actor overnight."

Coach Pete always had a 24/7 mentality about his work as a head coach. He figured that FSU would never lose a football game because the other coaching staff outworked his. When trying to convey to his players the importance of working hard, this statement which represents the finest in "Petersonese," just came out naturally. A fired up Coach Pete employed it to emphasize the importance of developing a good work ethic. He often pointed out the mindset a player must have to excel in football and life.

The President on Coach Peterson
T. K. Wetherell

T. K. Wetherell played for Bill Peterson (1965-'67).
Later he became Speaker of the State House of Representatives.
In 2003 he was appointed President of Florida State University.
He is still in the record books for a 100-yard kickoff return.

"Coach Pete called me and said, 'I have two scholarships available. One for you and one for that other fellow (Bill Moremen, RB from Daytona Beach). If Moremen doesn't come, don't bother to show up.'

"You didn't drop passes if you played for Coach Peterson. If you dropped it you were gone.

"The things I remember about Coach Peterson are the things he taught you about life in general, besides playing football. Running a university and trying to figure out how to get money from the state legislature is basically no different from trying to come up with a game plan to beat Florida."

Wetherell caught 35 passes before moving to defense where he intercepted three passes.

College Football's All-Time Biggest Winner
on Coach Peterson
Bobby Bowden

Bobby Bowden was a member of Peterson's staff (1963-'65). He returned to FSU as head coach in 1976 and became college football's all-time winningest coach with 373 wins through 2007.

"I would say, of my offensive philosophy, I would think 70% of it came from Bill Peterson. He was so far ahead of his time.

"Pete is the guy I got a lot of my trick plays from. Every game Pete had a trick play. He might even start the game with it.

"Pete would have an idea and his assistant coaches might not like it. They would get in an argument about it in a staff meeting and he would say, 'Wait a minute.' He would go to his office and call Sid Gilman (San Diego Chargers Coach). Then, he would come back and say, 'Gilman says we can do that, so we're doing it.'"

In 2008 Bobby Bowden coached in his 500th game. In 34 years at FSU, his Seminole teams have won over 300 games.

Pete's Practices

"YOU'VE GOT TO RUN A LITTLE MORE THAN FULL SPEED OUT THERE."

Peterson's Seminoles shocked the college football world with 48-6 upset of 5th ranked Kentucky on October 10, 1964.

"THIS WEEK WE'RE CHANGING THE FLOOR MAT AROUND HERE."

1964 Seminoles compiled 9-1-1 record under Pete, including a Gator Bowl win over Oklahoma, 36-19.

"I TELL YOU WHAT. YOU'VE GOT 13 WEEKS OF IT AND YOU'VE GOT NEXT WEEK, TOO."

Bill Peterson became the first Seminole coach to record 50 wins on September 20, 1969 with 24-0 shutout of Wichita State.

"IN THE GAME OF FOOTBALL YOU'VE GOT TO PIPE THE PLAYER."

In Bill Peterson's early years when the Seminoles took the field they were almost always outmanned by teams like Alabama, Georgia, Auburn and Georgia Tech, who had talented second- and third-string players almost as good as those on their starting unit. While FSU's starting lineup was good, talented depth was often a problem. Coach Pete constantly preached to his players that in order to compete with the big boys of college football, each individual player must realize he had to pay the price, although he didn't express it with the correct words.

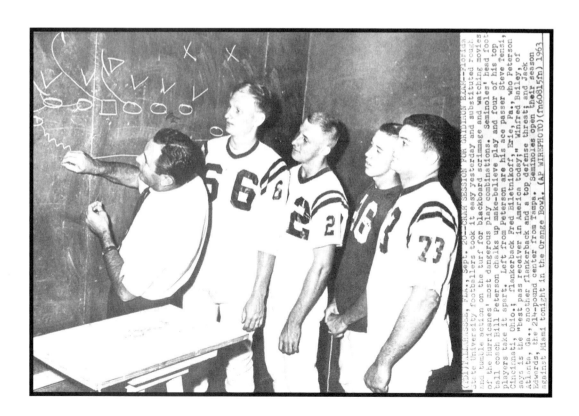

"WE'RE ALL IN THIS TOGETHER AND DON'T YOU REMEMBER IT."

The Seminoles, led by "Seven Magnificents", recorded shutouts in the first three games of the 1964 season.

"Now pair up in threes and line up in a circle."

Coach Peterson's recognition of coaching talent is evidenced by a dozen of his assistants who went on to head coaching positions in the NCAA and NFL.

"YOU GUYS LINE UP ALPHABETICALLY BY HEIGHT."

Former Peterson assistant coach Joe Gibbs ('67-'68) won three Super Bowls coaching the Washington Redskins for 16 years.

"MEN, I'VE TALKED TO A NUTRITIONIST AND I WANT TO TELL YOU SOMETHING. THREE THINGS ARE BAD FOR YOU. I CAN'T REMEMBER THE FIRST TWO, BUT THE THIRD IS DO-NUTS."

Peterson was the consummate worrier. He always worried about things that could adversely affect his team. One time he got wind of some bad eating habits being conducted by certain players. At that time the team's training table was closed down because of renovations to the cafeteria. The players had been given meal tickets so they could eat at the student union. There, without any football staff supervision, they were free to choose the food they wanted. Someone saw a few players consuming large numbers of donuts and reported it to the coach.

The Judge on Coach Peterson
Kim Hammond

Kim Hammond was involved in some of the most exciting games in Seminole football history. He quarterbacked the first FSU win at Florida, the amazing 37-37 tie of Bear Bryant's Alabama team and completed 37 passes in the Gator Bowl against Joe Paterno's Penn State team.
This All-American player later became Circuit Court Judge of Florida's Seventh Judicial District.

"Sure we were aware that Coach Pete messed up his words sometimes, but he never failed to communicate to me what he meant. Regardless of what he said, by his body language, by the spark in his eye, by the expression on his face, you didn't have to hear the words. You knew there was something going on.

"I don't remember anybody laughing at him. As the years went by we joked a little about it, but I never saw anybody express any disrespect or ridicule or do anything that gave evidence they lacked respect for him when he coached. Even if he said 'you're going to become a football overnight' we would all go try our best to become a football overnight."

As a senior, All-American
Kim Hammond
passed for 1,991 yards,
15 TDs and
scored twice rushing.

PETE AT GAMETIME

"Now I lay me down to sleep..."

A religious man, Coach Peterson told one of his five sons, Bill Peterson, Jr., that among his most treasured accomplishments was being elected president of his church's Sunday School class.

Always in a hurry, but mindful to stop and say a prayer before games, he told his team in the locker room at the Orange Bowl stadium before taking the field to play the Miami Hurricanes to bow their heads as he lead them in the Lord's Prayer.

T. K Wetherell remembers that Coach Pete inadvertently started uttering a childhood prayer and realized what he was doing. He stopped and turned to tight end "Red" Dawson who was standing next to him and said, "Red, you take it."

In 1964, Bill "Red" Dawson caught 12 passes, scored one TD, and was surprisingly called on to lead one prayer — before the Miami game. FSU won 14-0.

"I DIDN'T BRING YOU UP HERE ON A FOUR-PLANE ENGINE FOR NOTHING."

Bill Parcells, former linebacker coach under Pete, won two Super Bowls and coached five NFL teams: Giants, Jets, Patriots, Cowboys, and the Dolphins.

"Lead us in a few words of silent prayer."

One of Coach Peterson's more difficult requests. Once before a game he asked defensive end Ronnie Wallace to do this.

Studying to be ordained as a minister, Ronnie Wallace was the likely candidate to lead the team in prayer. But, he didn't play like a preacher. A quick, hard-hitting defensive end, Wallace recovered nine fumbles in his career.

"NOW WHEN THE COINS GO OUT FOR THE TOSS OF THE CAPTAINS..."

QB Eddie Feely (#14) and RB Keith Kinderman (#26) accounted for a combined 21 touchdowns in the 1961-1962 seasons.

"THINGS ARE NOT GOING GOOD OUT THERE AND THEY'VE GOT OUR WALLS TO THE BACK. BUT, WE'VE GOT TO KEEP OUR COOLS."

In Peterson's first game the Seminoles recorded a shutout in defeating Richmond, 28-0. The 1960 Seminoles held three opponents scoreless.

Pep Rally. 10/6/66.

1. THE GAME THIS WEEKEND REMINDS ME OF THE BOY NAMED JACK
   WHO CLIMBED THE BEANSTALK AND GOT THE GOLDEN EGG. THE
   GIANT CAME AFTER HIM AND JACK CUT DOWN THE BEANSTALK, KILLED
   THE GIANT AND GOT THE GOLDEN EGG.

2. THIS WEEKEND FLORIDA STATE HAS THE GOLDEN EGG.
   (1) IT'S A GOLDEN EGG WITH NATIONAL RANKING INSIDE.
   (2) THE TROUBLE IS FLORIDA HAS TO CLIMB OUR BEANSTALK TO
       GET IT.

3. NOT ONLY THAT - SATURDAY ISN'T GOING TO BE KIDS' DAY AND THE
   GAME ISN'T GOING TO HAVE A FAIRY TALE ENDING.
   (1) OUR MEN HAVE DECIDED NO ONE ELSE CLIMBS OUR BEANSTALK
       AND GETS A GOLDEN EGG.
   (2) WE KNOW FLORIDA IS #10.
   (3) WE KNEW KENTUCKY WAS #5 TWO YEARS AGO *BUT* THEY DIDN'T GET
       THE GOLDEN EGG.
   (4) WE KNEW GEORGIA WAS #5 LAST YEAR. *But* THEY DIDN'T GET THE
       GOLDEN EGG.

4. SO WE HAVE ONE PLAN FOR SATURDAY
   (1) WE PLAN TO SPANK JACK
   (2) SEND HIM HOME TO MOTHER
   (3) AND THE GIANT KEEPS THE GOLDEN EGG FOR HIMSELF.

**A copy of the Original notes typed and used by Coach Peterson at
a pep rally, two days before the infamous game with
the Florida Gators on October 8, 1966.**

"I'M NOT GOING TO TAKE THIS LOSS STANDING DOWN."

One of the toughest losses of all time for Peterson and Florida State came on October 8, 1966. Playing the arch rival Gators in Doak S. Campbell Stadium before a capacity home crowd, the Seminoles trailed by three points with 28-seconds remaining. The ball was resting on the Florida 45-yard line. Pete decided to go for broke and was successful —well, not really.

Quarterback Gary Pajcic lofted a pass that lanky Lane Fenner caught over his shoulder while falling to the ground in the end zone for the apparent winning touchdown. But, referee Doug Mosely, out-of-position to make the call according to Seminole fans, ruled that Fenner fell out of bounds before he secured the ball. Photographs clearly showed Fenner's knee on the ground, in the end zone.

Not only was this a hard loss for Peterson and the Seminoles to stomach, receiver T. K Wetherell refused to. Over thirty-years later, when Wetherell became president of the University, he went into the Florida State archives and put an asterisk next to the final score which he changed to reflect a 26-25 victory for FSU. He wasn't going to "take a loss standing down" either.

A picture is worth a thousand words!

Huff "The Magic Dragon" on Coach Peterson
Gary Huff

On October 10, 1970, FSU trailed the Gators 38-7 with seven minutes left. Sophomore QB Gary Huff came in and threw three TD passes in just over six minutes. The next week "Huff-The Magic Dragon" signs went up all over Tallahassee – a lighthearted takeoff of the popular song by Peter, Paul and Mary – "Puff the Magic Dragon."

"Coach Pete told me to go warm up in the middle of the third quarter. Dan Henning (Offensive coordinator) saw me and told me to go sit down."

This happened three different times. In the 4th quarter Huff was standing by Pete when FSU got the ball and was sent into the game. "Not only was that my first game action, I hadn't even run a play with the first unit in practice or even taken a snap from the center."

Huff promptly threw a 43- yard TD pass to Mike Gray, then two TD passes to Barry Smith, the last one a 66-yarder. He totaled 230 passing yards.

"I heard that Coach Peterson fired Henning after the game. But, he hired him back the next day.

"Coach Peterson was a man with a lot of energy. He was passionate about football. He had a good heart. He cared about his players. They were his kids.

"He was a disciplinarian. If a player got in trouble and the police came he would ask them to take him directly to jail and not call the coach.

"He said those malapropisms so smoothly they went right over your head. You would hardly notice them."

Tampa native Gary Huff set FSU passing records with over 6,000 yards and 54 touchdowns.

PETE'S PLAYER DESCRIPTIONS

"HERE'S ALL-AMERICAN WIDE RECEIVER... UH, UH, WELL YOU KNOW HIM... NUMBER 34!"

Ron Sellers caught 212 passes at Florida State, a record that still tops the "Career Receptions" category. Governor Claude Kirk (R) was impressed.

The All Time Great Receiver
Ron Sellers

Ron Sellers, the pass catching-phenom from Jacksonville, FL broke every existing record for receivers during his three years as a starter. So outstanding was his success that 15 of his records remained tops in the Seminole record book beginning the 2009 season.

The stories are legendary about Sellers, who was dubbed "Jingle Joints" because of his tall, lean looks by a Houston Cougar defender whose tongue was hanging out from chasing him all game. Sellers was a game-breaking, consensus All-American whose name was known far and wide by everyone in Seminole Territory except apparently Coach Peterson.

At the PowWow, the traditional Friday night Homecoming celebration, Peterson introduced the seniors to the crowd. Each player was wearing his game jersey with his number on it, but unfortunately for Coach Pete, back then the jerseys did not have players' names on them.

When it came time to introduce Sellers, Pete blanked out on his name, but was undaunted because he knew everybody would know this famous player – by number, anyway.

On October 26, 1968 Ron Sellers caught 16 passes in a 35-28 victory at South Carolina. This single game record still stands.

"FRED BILETNIKOFF'S LIMITATIONS ARE LIMITLESS. HE'S FOOTSURE AND FANCY FREE!"

Fred Biletnikoff pictured here with Peterson and TE Red Dawson caught 13 passes in the 1965 Gator Bowl against Oklahoma.

"HE'S A TRICK OF ALL TRADES."

The trickster Tommy Warren passed for over 1,600 yards and 11 touchdowns in 1970.

"HE DIDN'T HAVE A GOOD SPRING PRACTICE BECAUSE HE WAS SLOWED BY AMMONIA PART OF THE TIME."

Paul Magalski, object of pre-season health concerns, averaged over six yards per carry in 1969.

"HE HAS A CHRONICLE KNEE INJURY."

Despite an injury-hampered career, Cairo speedster Larry Green scored seven rushing touchdowns and added three receiving passes.

"HE HAS ONE OF THOSE NAGGRAVATING INJURIES THAT JUST SEEM TO HANG ON."

Gary Pajcic (#16), pictured here with Coach Pete and Bill Cappleman (#14), overcame injuries to pass for over 1,500 yards in 1966.

Quarterback on Coach Pete
Steve Tensi

Cincinnati native Steve Tensi caught Bill Peterson's eye and was lured to Tallahassee where he helped take the passing game to a new level. His career record of 275 completed passes for 3,697 yards and 33 touchdowns earned him a spot in the Florida State Hall of Fame.

"I told a guy one time that Bill Peterson was the Elvis Presley of college football.

"He was the first one to make it a big time commodity at Florida State. It seems to me before Coach Peterson got there people were trying to get Florida State on their schedule for homecoming games so they could beat them up by about 51-0. When Coach Pete changed us from being a running team to one that would pass more than 50% of the time, we stopped getting those homecoming invitations.

"So, you have to give Bill Peterson a lot of credit. Looking at the things he said some people might have thought he was a dummy. He wasn't. He was dumb like a fox."

In the 1965 Gator Bowl, Steve Tensi passed for 303 yards with five touchdowns. That performance put the finishing touch on an NFL offer from the Baltimore Colts and another from the AFL's San Diego Chargers.

PETE'S PHILOSOPHY

"I'VE ALWAYS HAD GREAT REPERTOIRE WITH MY PLAYERS."

Red Dawson (#83) later coached at Marshall University. He went on a recruiting trip and was not on the flight of the fatal plane crash that inspired the 2006 hit movie; "We are Marshall." Red's role in the movie was played by Matthew Fox.

"MEN, WE'RE GOING OUT THERE AND FILL THE FOOTBALLS WITH AIR!"

These guys had lots of air-filled football stuff to reminisce about. From left to right, former Florida State Head Football coaches include: Ed Williamson (1947); Don Veller (1948-'52); Bobby Bowden (1976-2009); Bill Peterson (1960-'70).

"Just remember the words of Henry Patrick: 'Kill me or let me live.'"

Maybe it was Coach Peterson's ability to quote famous people that made him popular with Florida's Governors like Haydon Burns ('65-'67), on the far right, and Farris Bryant ('61-'65) between Pete and Burns.

"DON'T LOOK A SAWHORSE IN THE MOUTH."

On November 29, 1968, Pete's Seminoles shocked the favored Houston Cougars in Jacksonville, 40-20. The stunning victory secured a spot in the inaugural Peach Bowl against LSU and the third consecutive Bowl appearance by FSU.

"LIKE TWO SHIPS THAT CRASH IN THE NIGHT."

QB competitors Ed Pritchett (#16) and Steve Tensi (#13) combined to complete 400 passes for over 4,000 yards and 35 touchdowns.

"DON'T BURN YOUR BRIDGES AT BOTH ENDS."

Forty-seven of Coach Peterson's Seminoles signed professional football contracts.

"LET SLEEPING BAGS LIE."

Bill Peterson was the father of five – all boys.

"LET A DEAD HORSE REST."

**Peterson with UF Coach Ray Graves.
Florida State defeated the University of Florida, 16-7,
in the Gators first visit to Tallahassee,
on November 21, 1964.**

"NOBODY GOES TO THE SILVER SLIPPER ANYMORE, IT'S TOO CROWDED."

For Pete's sake, it's only a basketball game. Might as well figure out where to go for dinner afterwards.

"I'M THE FOOTBALL AROUND HERE AND DON'T YOU REMEMBER IT."

"But Coach, do you remember my first year as a starter – 1968 – when I passed for 2,410 yards, 25 TDs, and made All-American?"
- Bill Cappleman

"A ROLLING PIN GATHERS NO MOSS."

Always in perpetual motion like their leader, Coach Pete's teams scored more than 20 points in 53 games. On 12 occasions they scored in the 30s and in 10 games tallied 40 or more points.

"DON'T KILL THE GOOSE THAT LAID THE DEVILED EGG."

Inheriting a troubled football program, Bill Peterson took his teams to four bowl games. In the 23 years prior to his arrival the Seminoles had only made three bowl appearances.

"NO GUNS AT ANY TIME IN THE DORM — WE DON'T WANT ANY HUNTERMEN AROUND."

Avid hunter Dan Whitehurst from Adel, GA was a head-hunting linebacker at Florida State. In the first game of the '70 season he blocked a Louisville FG attempt to preserve the win. He would also record 96 tackles and two interceptions that season.

"WE CAN HANG OUR HEADS HIGH."

The script for the ABC television documentary on Bear Bryant, being filmed on September 23, 1967, was re-written by the Seminoles, who came from behind four times to fashion a 37-37 win… uh, tie.

"JUST REMEMBER BUDDY, OUR CROSSES WILL PATH AGAIN."

Peterson worked so hard to establish FSU's football program on a national level he was never happy when an assistant coach left to take a job with another team, especially at another college. Perhaps, this call is to Ken Meyer, who left FSU to run the offense at Alabama where Joe Namath and Ken Stabler became quarterbacks. Coincidentally, his offense would go against Pete's in the famous 37-37 tie game in 1967 at Tuscaloosa.

Peterson was the offensive line coach and a top recruiter at LSU before coming to Florida State. Under his watch the Tigers won the national championship in 1958.

"YOU AIN'T GONNA DEPUTIZE MY JOB."

Peterson's staff meetings were lively affairs as they hammered out game strategies. Always open to new ideas, Coach Pete was fine with brainstorming a situation to come up with the best solution. Bobby Bowden remembered that sometimes an argument would crop up over whether an idea suggested by an assistant coach would work or not. In those situations Pete would put his foot down and say that he would not deputize, uh… jeopardize his job by trying to make a strategy work that was destined to fail.

Some of the more heated sessions concerned strategies for handling the Gators.

"YOU CAN OBSERVE A LOT BY WATCHING."

Dan Henning, Pete's Offensive Chief, '68-'70, served as Head Coach of Falcons ('83-'86) and Chargers ('89-'91).

Record Setting QB on Coach Pete
Bill Cappleman

After patiently waiting his turn, Bill Cappleman took over the Seminole offense in 1968 and over the next two years completed 349 passes for 4,904 yards and 39 touchdowns. He was an All-American who was drafted in the second round by the Minnesota Vikings.

"Even though Coach Peterson sometimes put his mouth in motion before his mind was in gear, everybody who played for him had an enormous amount of respect for him. For example, we were watching game film and one of his assistants called attention to something that should have been whistled by an official. Coach Pete said, 'Jimmimany Cricket' instead of Jiminy Cricket.

"But, he was an excellent motivator because football was what he loved and he put everything into it. He got excited, no doubt about it. He was a player's coach."

Apparently Bill Cappleman listened well. Over 40 years later he was still listed in the top 10 in the record books for:

  Most passing yards in a game
  Career completions
  Season TD passes
  Career TD passes

Linebacker on Coach Pete
Dick Hermann

Dick Hermann parlayed toughness and quickness into a place in the Florida State Hall of Fame. He was a leader on the famous defensive unit named "The Seven Magnificents" in 1964. Hermann played his best in big games and was signed to a pro contract with the Oakland Raiders.

"Coach Peterson is remembered most as an offensive coach but he helped develop the Chinese Bandits defensive unit at LSU. Peterson, if he was anything, was a defensive genius. He molded the defense first, then the offense caught up."

"He did mix up his words at times especially when it came to names. One player whose name he never could get right was Bobby Menendez. I remember watching Coach on his television show one time and he called Menendez 'Munoz' and everything else except his real name."

Florida State

DICK HERMANN

> All American Dick Hermann
> recorded eight tackles in
> Seminoles 14-0 shutout of Miami
> Hurricanes, September 19, 1964.

PETE'S UPDATES

"THE WAY I PLAY GOLF I'D SET THE GAME BACK 100 YARDS."

Billy Sexton
on Pete the Golfer

Billy Sexton was a QB at Florida State who returned as an assistant coach for 30 years and now works for Seminole Boosters, Inc. As a QB Coach he tutored Jimmy Jordan and Wally Woodham. Then he coached running backs for 24 years, turning out many successful NFL RB's including Warrick Dunn and Greg Jones.

Billy had a memorable golfing experience playing in the foursome behind Coach Peterson's group one summer's day. He was standing on the tee for the 13th hole at Winewood Golf Course (now Hilamin) as Coach Peterson attempted his second shot. He remembers very clearly what happened next.

"The 13th is a dog left, up a hill, a tough par five," Sexton said. "From about 20 yards past the tee up to almost 350 yards there is a big lake on the left, so you have to worry about your ball going into the water.

"Coach Peterson had hit a ball that settled about four or five feet from the edge of the water. So, he had to stand on the edge of the lake, with his back to the water, and the ball was above his feet. He had on a wide-brimmed hat and a cigar in his mouth.

"He made a vicious swing at the ball, which went up the fairway, but he lost his balance and his arms were flailing around, looked like the Lipton Tea commercial. He was kind of in suspended animation for two or three seconds, seemed like forever, and he fell back into the lake.

"He went under, was submerged, but he came right back up. Didn't miss a beat. Still had the hat on and the cigar in his mouth. He was dripping water, completely drenched, water was even sloshing out of his shoes. He just walked on off after his ball.

"All of us were dying laughing. Couldn't play the next two holes we were laughing so hard. That's all we talked about for the next two weeks."

Talk about learning from the Legends of the Game. Billy Sexton (R) played under Bear Bryant and coached with Bobby Bowden.

"HOW SHOULD I KNOW IF IT IS GOING TO RAIN OR NOT. I'M NOT A GEOLOGIST."

The weather was very predictable on September 20, 1969. An all day rain turned Doak Campbell Stadium into a quagmire, resulting in 24 fumbles. Wichita State fumbled 17 times. FSU recovered 10. Bill Cappleman's two touchdown passes led the Seminoles to a 24-0 win in this season opener of college football's 100th season.

"IT'S GOING TO BE A GREAT GAME TONIGHT. WE HAVE THE TWO NATION'S GREATEST LINEMEN."

In his role as analyst on the Seminole Radio broadcast Bill Peterson provided lots of color with his interesting mix of strategy and strategic malapropisms. On October 11, 1980, Coach Pete worked the Florida State-Pittsburgh game in Tallahassee. The Seminoles were ranked 11th in the AP Poll after upsetting Nebraska the previous week. The Panthers were ranked 4th. Many of the players in this game, including Dan Marino, would end up in the NFL. The two players who excited Peterson most were defensive linemen: FSU's Ron Simmons and Pitt's Hugh Green. The Seminoles won the game, 36-22.

Two-time Consensus All-American Ron Simmons recorded 25 career QB sacks on the way to the Hall of Fame.

"Florida State lost all their minimum before half-time."

Bill Peterson, color analyst on the Seminole Radio Network, summed up a game by explaining how the home team got themselves in a hole in the first half.

"Fools fall in where angels fear to tread."

This may not be what Coach Peterson and FSU President Stanley Marshall were talking about, but it's a good observation anyway.

"I USED TO HAVE THIS SPEECH IMPLEMENT AND COULDN'T REMEMBER THINGS BEFORE I TOOK THAT SAM CARNEGIE COURSE."

Pete got his message across when his teams were scheduled to play Miami. His 'Noles beat the 'Canes all five times they met between 1963-'70.

"WHEN OUR LITTLE BOYS SAW THE INSIDE OF THAT ASTRONOMICAL DOME THEIR EYES GOT AS BIG AS SAUSAGES."

Former Governors Claude Kirk (L) (1967-'71) and
LeRoy Collins (R) (1955-'61) always enjoyed
a good Peterson story.

"WHEW, THAT WAS A CLIFF-DWELLER TO END ALL CLIFF-DWELLERS."

Peterson with legendary Michigan State Coach Daugherty.
"Well Duffy you ain't heard nothing yet.
Wait 'til I tell you about our game against Alabama and the Bear."

PETE'S PEARLS

"Look at that quarterback, he can throw with either hand. He's amphibious."

Billy Sexton recalled the story of what was taking place in the stands while he was Quarterbacking the Leon Lions High School team against Gainesville High. Because of the high interest in this game, which was viewed by some as a matchup of the Seminoles against the Gators, since it was a Tallahassee school against one from Gainesville, the game was played in Doak S. Campbell Stadium in the Capital City.

The story goes that Coach Peterson was sitting in the stands with a couple of his assistant coaches who were scouting players to recruit for FSU. Sexton said, "Eddie McAshan, the GHS QB was apparently ambidextrous. In the pre-game warm-ups he ran a play to the right side and threw a pass right-handed. Then, he ran one to the left and threw a pass left-handed. When Peterson saw that he turned to one of his assistants and said, 'Did you see that? The QB can throw with either hand, he's amphibious.'"

A side note: Georgia Tech signed McAshan to a scholarship, where he became the first African-American QB to start at a major southeastern university. He threw 32 TD passes, but also set a record by throwing 51 interceptions.

"WE'RE GOING TO THROW THE FOOTBALL COME HIGH OR HELL WATER. WE'RE NOT GOING TO BE ANY THREE CLOUDS AND A YARD-OF-DUST TEAM."

Coach Pete's teams passed for over 21,000 yards and 45 touchdowns!

"WE CAN BEAT THIS TEAM. ALL WE HAVE TO DO IS CAPITALIZE ON OUR MISTAKES."

By 1964 Pete's prolific passing attack began to take off featuring the Tensi to Biletnikoff combination. In this 9-1-1 season the future Hall of Fame receiver had 100+ yards in receiving in seven games and caught 11 Tensi throws for TDs.

"LET'S NIP THIS THING IN THE BUTT."

Tom Haney and Doug Henderson have been the Florida State team physicians since 1975. Haney was in Bill Peterson's first group of players. He caught a pass in the FSU-Florida freshman game in which the Seminoles beat the Gators for the first time, 35-10.

"I GUARANTEE YOU THEY ARE DOWN THERE, JUST BLOCKING THEIR CHIPS... UH, CHOPPING THEIR LOCKS, I MEAN LICKING THEIR CHOPS."

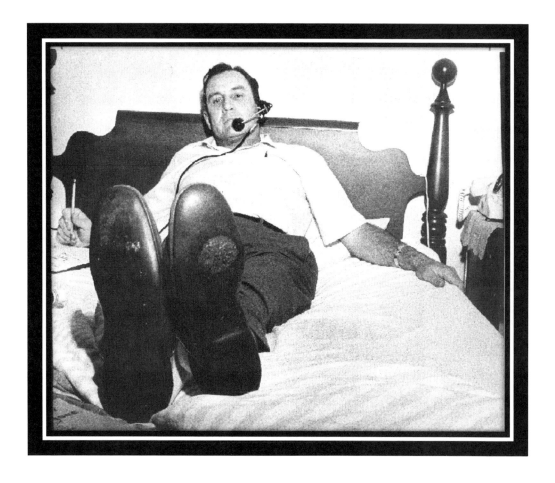

Pete's 1967 Seminoles defeated the Gators 21-16 in Gainesville.
It was their seventh consecutive victory guaranteeing them
a berth in the Gator Bowl against Penn State.

"WHERE YOU BEEN; OUT BOGGIN'?"

Noticing a couple of his younger coaches coming into the gym looking sweaty, Pete deduced that they had been out running. Two of the younger coaches in this photo are in the first row: Don James, far left, and Bobby Bowden, far right.

"THAT VERBAL COMMITMENT AIN'T WORTH THE PAPER IT'S WRITTEN ON."

Bob Harbison was a member of Coach Peterson's staff every year. He started at Florida State as a member of Don Veller's 1948 staff and worked with every Seminole Head Coach until he retired in 1985. "Harby" soon learned that he needed to come back from a recruiting trip with a signed, not a spoken, agreement. Pete didn't trust those "verbal commitments." While recruiting in Jacksonville in 1966, he ran out of grant-in-aid forms, called Pete, and was told to make a photocopy to sign a player by the name of Ron Sellers, who looked more like a "basketball player than a football player."

Bob Harbison, the former Indiana lineman, became a renowned line coach at Florida State. His most famous unit was the fierce group he coached under Peterson in 1964 called the "Seven Magnificents." Harby was voted into the FSU Hall of Fame in 1987.

"Wayne McDuffie left Florida State. He got a job with the Atlantic Falcons."

Seminole assistant coach Billy Sexton was on a trip and he bumped into Bill Peterson in the airport. Coach Pete, eager to bring Billy up-to-date on the latest news from Seminole territory, revealed he had heard that FSU's offensive coordinator had accepted a position with an NFL team. Pete said he was hired by the Atlantic Falcons. Smiling, Coach Sexton wondered if there was a new team in the NFL.

Wayne McDuffie played on three of Coach Peterson's bowl teams: two Gator Bowls and a Sun Bowl. The Hawkinsville, GA native lettered on offense and defense. Later he returned as Offensive Coordinator for Bobby Bowden, 1983-'89.

"DOC, YOU'RE NOT GOING TO STICK ONE OF THOSE RVS IN ME, ARE YOU?"

For the major part of his life Bill Peterson was blessed with robust health. As this changed in his later years, he questioned what the doctor would be doing. He wasn't sure he wanted one of those IVs stuck in his arm. An RV would be even worse.

The Son
Bill Peterson Jr.

Bill Peterson Jr. was the fourth of five sons born to Bill and Marge Peterson. He said they named him Bill Jr. because they had run out of boys names. He learned his love of football from his Dad and currently serves as Athletic Director and Running Backs Coach for Shorter College in Rome, Georgia.

–"Even though Dad had five sons he looked at his football team as sons #6 through 106."

–"Always thought he had the ability of pulling people together in the same direction."

–"He couldn't go anywhere in Tallahassee whether it was shopping at Nic's Toggery or to a restaurant that people didn't recognize him."

–"He was a very strong Christian. Dad started the first FCA group at FSU."

–"He decided he would just go along with the funny sayings attributed to him and not get angry about it. At times he did put people on. He got inducted into the Florida Sports Hall of Fame at a time when the Nixon indictments, Haldeman, and others were in the news. He told me he was going to say he was proud to be 'indicted' into the Hall of Fame."

–"When he was offered the 49ers job there was a sign on the bank near our house that said: '**Don't Go Coach Pete**'. When he turned down the job they changed the sign to read: '**Thanks Coach Pete, We Love You!**'"

–"I would hope he would be remembered as an innovator. Someone who changed the course of history for Florida State in football and as a University."

Monday, January 8, 1968
Excerpt from Tallahassee Democrat Editorial
By Malcom Johnson

TALLAHASSEE, FL–Football at Florida State University is vital in the ultimate analysis mainly as it stands as a symbol of excellence. Excellence in any moral endeavor justifies itself. Under Coach Bill Peterson the FSU Seminoles have achieved a state of excellence on the intercollegiate gridiron.

PETE'S ACCOLADES

"THE GREATEST THING JUST HAPPENED. I GOT INDICTED INTO THE FLORIDA SPORTS HALL OF FAME."

While attending school at Ohio Northern University, Peterson worked at the Wilson Football Factory in Ada, Ohio. His job was to turn footballs inside-out in the manufacturing process. So, Pete could truthfully say he knew football "inside-out."

"THEY GAVE ME A STANDING OBSERVATION."

Pete tells Governor Farris Bryant how
one of his own speeches had been received.

PETE IN THE NFL

"Men, I want you to remember one word and one word only, and that word is: super bowl."

After leaving Florida State University to coach at Rice University for a year, Bill Peterson then turned his attention to the National Football League. This fulfilled a lifetime dream. Marge Peterson said: "Bill had always wanted to be a Pro coach. That was his aim in life."

Unfortunately during his brief time with the Houston Oilers his quotes were more memorable than his accomplishments. One that has outlasted all the others was his instruction to the team on the first day of practice when he gathered the players at mid-field and told them to focus their thinking on THE WORD "Super Bowl."

Okay, so that's two words. He still got his point across.

Peterson's Bowl Tradition

Year	Bowl	Opponent	Score
1964	Gator	Oklahoma	36-19 (W)
1966	Sun	Wyoming	20-28 (L)
1967	Gator	Penn State	17-17 (T)
1968	Peach	LSU	27-31 (L)

"I WANT YOU MEN STANDING ON YOUR HELMETS WITH THE SIDELINE UNDER YOUR ARMS."

Instructions on being prepared to play the game of football begins at an early age with the same advice Pete gave to his NFL players.

"THAT OAKLAND IS TOUGH. THEY TIMIDATE YOUR OFFENSE. THEY TIMIDATE YOUR DEFENSE. THEY EVEN TIMIDATE THE OFFICIALS."

Coach Bill Peterson and sportswriter Bill McGrotha stayed in touch after Pete left Tallahassee. When the two talked before Peterson's Houston Oilers played the Oakland Raiders, Pete expressed his misgivings about that upcoming game.

VS.

Unfortunately Coach Peterson's assessment of the Raiders was accurate. They defeated the Oilers, 34-0, on October 9, 1972 during Monday Night Football.

PETE'S DEMOCRACY

Pete's Fuzzy Math:

"MEN WE'VE JUST BEEN INVITED TO PLAY IN THE SUN BOWL IN EL PASO, TEXAS ON CHRISTMAS EVE. NOW WE CAN GO TO THE BOWL OR WE CAN GO ON HOME FOR THE CHRISTMAS HOLIDAYS."

The team voted and only four or five players voted to accept the bowl bid which prompted Coach Pete to say:

"OKAY, IT'S UNANIMOUS. WE'RE GOING TO THE SUN BOWL."

"Each of you players will receive a nice piece of Seminite luggage."

To make his team feel better about the Sun Bowl vote, Coach Pete told them about the benefit. They wouldn't be home for Christmas, but "gosh," they would get luggage!

2/24/66, Sun Bowl, El Paso, Tx

From the Tallahassee Democrat, 12/25/1966,
By Bill McGrotha

*EL PASO, TX - **Kim Hammond** came off the bench to throw three touchdown passes for Florida State, but it wasn't enough to handle Wyoming's really fierce Cowboys, who fought from behind and won 28-20 here Saturday in the 32nd annual Sun Bowl.*

....

*Checked without a first down in the opening quarter, FSU tied it on Hammond's 49-yard bomb to **Ron Sellers**. Soon after the Seminoles went ahead 14-7 as **T.K. Wetherell** converted a short sidelines pass from Hammond into a spectacular 59-yard payoff.*

The Seminoles got the luggage but not the Bowl victory!

"WE'RE GOING TO HAVE A GRAND TIME, BUT I DON'T WANT YOU GUYS GETTING IN TROUBLE OVER IN WARSAW."

Sage Sun Bowl advice from the Head Coach about crossing the border to Juarez, Mexico!

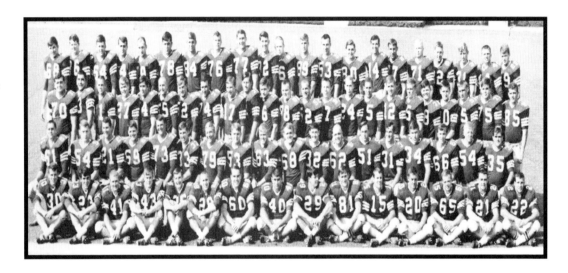

The 1966 Seminoles

Despite two TD catches by Ron Sellers, one from Gary Pajcic and the other from Kim Hammond, the Seminoles lost by eight points to the Jim Kiick-led Wyoming Cowboys in the Sun Bowl. Sellers had six receptions for 160 yards.

MORE

PETERSONISMS

As told to
Tallahassee Democrat's
Legendary Columnist

Bill McGrotha

For more than 30 years, Bill McGrotha chronicled the trials and tribulations of Florida State sports with a caring hand. A football game was not complete for FSU fans until the Sunday morning after when they had read what McGrotha had to say.

The Florida State Press Box is now named in his honor.

The Sportswriter
Bill McGrotha

The person who Bill Peterson trusted most in the media was Tallahassee Democrat sports columnist Bill McGrotha. They spent many hours conversing about a variety of subjects, but most of their time was spent talking about their favorite subject: Florida State Football.

McGrotha wrote a comprehensive history of FSU football: **Seminoles: The First Forty Years.** This book, which is now out of print, contained many of Coach Peterson's humorous sayings, strategies, and stories in a year-by-year breakdown of Pete's stay at Florida State.

In 1981, Gerald Ensley, Democrat writer and long-time friend, edited a book of McGrotha's columns entitled: **From the Sidelines: The Best of Bill McGrotha.** In a 1989 article McGrotha wrote about Peterson's indictment, uh, induction into the Florida Sports Hall of Fame:

> *"There is a malaprop-spinning part of Peterson that has always been amusingly different. But, it is great testimony to the serious worth of this man that more than 600 people are paying $50 tonight [to honor him]."*

Bill McGrotha left a big hole in the sports community when he passed away in January 1993. The hole became even wider and deeper when McGrotha's friend Bill Peterson left us seven months later.

Bill McGrotha presents Tallahassee QB Club award to Ron Sellers (L) and Kim Hammond.

"I'M SEEING MY LAWYER AND THIS IS GOING TO BE A SUIT CASE."

On October 14, 1961, playing in front of a capacity crowd that included 90 state legislators, Pete's charges shut out the Georgia Bulldogs, 3-0, in a hard-hitting defensive battle.

"HE HEARS FOOTPRINTS."

Coach Peterson came to this conclusion after trying to figure out why one of his receivers was having difficulty holding onto passes thrown to him over the middle.

"THEY GAVE HIM ONE OF THOSE E.G.G.s AND HAVE HIM IN INTENSIVE CARE."

Maybe Coach Pete was talking about Bill McGrotha, shown here presiding over an event honoring the Coach. McGrotha passed away from a heart attack in January of 1993. Peterson died seven months later, in August of 1993.

"HE DOESN'T EVEN ASSEMBLE A FOOTBALL PLAYER."

Always excitable during a game, it was reported that during half-time of one particular game that the Seminoles were losing. Coach Peterson was especially displeased with the play of a particular player. He approached Bobby Jackson, the assistant coach who had recruited the player, wondering how he could have signed such a player to a scholarship. Then he delivered a parting shot telling Jackson that he knew what he had been doing instead of finding top players. He said, "You been hanging out with your crownies up in Georgia."

Bobby Jackson (4th from left, front row) coached in the NFL for over 20 years with the Falcons, Chargers, Cardinals, Redskins, Rams and Dolphins. He served on Bill Peterson's FSU Staff from 1965-'69.

"RECRUITING TOP FOOTBALL PLAYERS. THAT IS THE CRUTCH OF THE PROBLEM."

Coach Pete signing up a new "Seminole" always provided a good photo op. Peterson sold recruits on the idea of achieving "firsts" because Florida State had a relatively new football program.

Two of Peterson's recruits, Fred Biletnikoff and Ron Sellers, are in the College Football Hall of Fame.

"The trouble with you sports writers is that you're always making me look dumb. You know I don't need any help."

Bill Peterson was a hit with the press. He always enjoyed bantering back and forth with the writers. Some of his most priceless Petersonisms came out in these exchanges.

Often he didn't even realize that he had created a malapropism until he read about it in the newspaper the next day. He remained undaunted by these little jabs that were taken at him in print, realizing that no one was out to get him per se.

He would kid around with the reporters to the extent that sometimes they had to question whether a phrase that seemed like a malapropism was an unintentional slip by Coach Peterson or he was simply playing with them. They couldn't be absolutely certain if he was "putting them on" or not. Just as he was a master at keeping an opponent's defense confused, he liked to befuddle the press at times.

When he told them that they "were trying to make him look dumb, but he didn't need any help" it seemed like that was his way of joking with them... or was it?

Tallahassee Democrat's Bill McGrotha (L) and Gainesville Sun's Jack Hairston were a couple of long-time sports columnists.

The Wife
Marge Peterson Remembers Life with Coach Pete

"When we were starting out in Ohio, I was a teacher and Bill was coaching from 8 a.m. to 10 p.m. He made $800 a year and I made $900. We thought we were really doing well.

"Bill had an uncle who used to take him to see the Pittsburgh Steelers play when he was a kid. Way back in those days he said, 'I want to be a football coach, no matter what happens.'

"The secret as to why Bill always had so much energy is that he would come home for lunch and I would make him a sandwich. After that he would take a 15-minute nap, then he was on the road again. He always said he could go all day long if he had his nap.

"He was different. If he went into a room full of strangers they would all know who he was when he left. He would shake everybody's hand.

"He was not a tremendous speaker and got his words mixed up at times. Part of that was because he had a very poor grammar school education where he grew up in southern West Virginia.

"Before a Miami game the kids were so nervous Bill decided to calm them down with a prayer. That's when he started out, 'Now I lay me down to sleep' and they were all laughing so much they weren't nervous anymore."

The Tie that Binds
On Sunday Morning, October 1, 1961, the opening hymn sung in Marge and Bill Peterson's Sunday School Class at Trinity United Methodist Church was "Blest Be the Tie That Binds." The day before the Seminoles had tied the Gators, 3-3. In 2008, Marge Peterson is still a member of that same class and each Sunday they close the class meeting with that same hymn.

PETERSON:
THE FAMILY MAN

"MARGE IS TRYING TO LOSE WEIGHT. SHE'S JOINED ONE OF THOSE NEW NIGHT WATCHERS CLUBS."

Bill and Marge

"IT'S COLD OUTSIDE, BE SURE TO PUT YOUR EAR MUFFINS ON."

You laugh, but where Peterson grew up you would freeze your, uh… ears off if you weren't prepared for the frigid weather.

Bill Peterson's best Christmas sent December, 1963

One Christmas in particular stands out in my memory, because it proved to me and my family that geography has no real bearing on the Christmas spirit.

It was my first year as assistant football coach at Louisiana State University in Baton Rouge. Having been raised in Ohio, we were accustomed to snow and the sound of sleigh bells during the Christmas season. Somehow, the warm Louisiana nights and a holiday mood didn't quite fit together.

Several transplanted Northern families had gathered at our house for mutual consolation. We were thinking of the snow and excitement of Christmas at home, and feeling sorry for ourselves in our present strange surroundings, when we heard the sound of Christmas carols being sung outside. We looked out, and there was a group of children dressed in shorts. Some were even barefooted.

They sang: "I'm dreaming of a white Christmas," and I suppose they were. After they left, we sat back and dreamed of the white Christmases we had known. Somehow, however, we felt better about the situation.

An original Christmas Story by Bill Peterson in his own typing.

Bill Peterson Becomes A Seminole

1 p.m. Dec 7, 1959

Bill Peterson, 39-year-old top assistant coach at Louisiana State University, is the new head football coach at Florida State University, FSU Director of Athletics Vaughn Mancha announced today.

Peterson accepted a four-year contract at a salary of $14,000 a year.

The announcement of the appointment of Peterson came 20 days after Perry Moss resigned to accept a position as head coach and general manager of the professional Montreal Alouettes.

"Coach Peterson has an outstanding background in football," Mancha said in making the announcement. "We are confident he will give us the progressive football program we visualize at Florida State University."

Peterson, offensive line coach at Louisiana State for the past four years, becomes Florida State's fifth modern-day head football coach. The Seminoles completed their 13th modern football season Nov. 28 with a 4-6 record.

Dean Mode L. Stone, chairman of Florida State's athletic committee which worked with Mancha in making the recommendation of Peterson to University President Robert M. Strozier, said "we feel we have selected a competent coach, a fine Christian gentleman, and a man that players, students, faculty, alumni, and friends shall appreciate."

Stone and Mancha said the athletic committee examined the qualifications of "a great number" of coaches throughout the country. A select number of coaches were interviewed in Tallahassee at the invitation of the committee.

"After thorough examination of all available information," Mancha said, "we unanimously recommended to President Strozier the name of Bill Peterson."

Peterson's name will be formally presented to the Florida Board of Control in Jacksonville Friday.

"I am very much pleased with the selection of Mr. Peterson," Strozier said.

(MORE)

**This is the original press release naming Bill Peterson
as Head Coach at Florida State University.**

"I have met Coach Peterson and he is a splendid person. The athletic committee and Mr. Mancha have done an outstanding job," Strozier said.

Peterson has been credited with obtaining many of the players who have boosted Louisiana State into the top ranks of collegiate football. LSU's 1958 team won the national championship and defeated Clemson in the 1959 Sugar Bowl. The 1959 Tigers compiled a 9-1 record and will meet the University of Mississippi in the Sugar Bowl on Jan. 1.

"Peterson has outstanding technical knowledge of football and has gained a fine reputation as a recruiter of student-athletes," Mancha said.

Contacted at Baton Rouge, Peterson said he is "simply elated" at his selection.

"I am delighted to have this opportunity of coaching at one of the finest \versities in the country," Peterson said. "I look forward to working with the Department of Athletics and administration at Florida State."

There was no indication today if Peterson would bring any assistant coaches with him to Florida State.

A major-college independent, Florida State will play a 10-game 1960 schedule that calls for games with Richmond, Florida, Wake Forest, The Citadel, Mississippi Southern, William and Mary, Kentucky, Miami, Houston, and Auburn.

A native of Toronto, O., Peterson went to LSU in 1955 after a successful tenure at Mansfield, O., High School. He also coached at Wapakoneta and Forest high schools in Ohio.

Peterson was graduated from Ohio Northern University, where he was a standout end in football. He is a Methodist Sunday School Superintendent in Baton Rouge.

Peterson and his wife, Marjorie, have five sons, ages 16, 11, 7, 3, and 2.

####### ############

"Those of us who loved him and were his friends are better off for having known him. Bill Peterson's death left a void in many of us. It also bequeathed us a legacy of love, humor and just plain goodness that will always remain in our lives."

-Vaughn Mancha

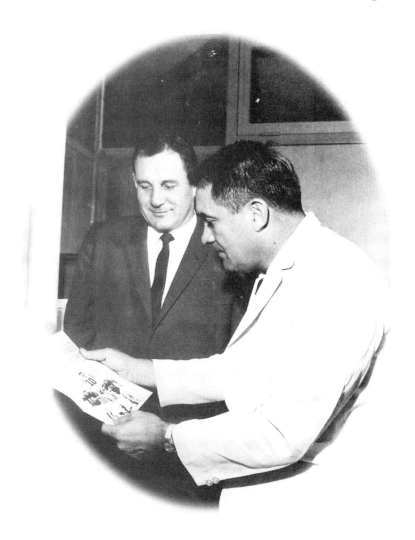

Athletic Director Vaughn Mancha

Remembering Pete
at the Silver Slipper

In his retirement, Bill Peterson put his friendliness and charm to work in raising funds for the Gus A. Stavros Center at Florida State University. The Stavros Center assists public schools and communities in the Big Bend area in furthering economic education and free enterprise. The Center honored Pete's memory and his work with a banquet at the Silver Slipper on August 28, 2000. Marge, Ron and Bill Peterson Jr. were in attendance. Here are a few of the stories told about the famous coach.

Bobby Bowden: "Just to show you how fate plays a part, I was head coach at Howard (now Samford), a small college in Birmingham. I was invited to a QB club meeting in Atlanta, one of the oldest in the country, with about 3,000 members. Because the club president graduated from Howard, I was seated next to Bill Peterson at the head table. We struck up a conversation and he asked me if I would be interested in a job."

T.K. Wetherell: "Coach Pete was pretty creative. In recruiting he promised me I would be on the first team if I would sign up. There were no scholarship limitations. There were 164 players when I got here. We took up two fields. I looked at the depth chart and sure enough I was on the first team… on the second page."

Dan Whitehurst: "Coach Peterson was an influential person who knew how to use his pull. FSU was put on the map when he was here. He recruited me and in 1967 I was also recruited by Alabama and went to a game there. FSU tied them. I was recruited by Houston and went to the game in Jacksonville. FSU beat them 40-20. Penn State recruited me and I went to the Gator Bowl; FSU tied them. The Seminoles also beat Spurrier. So I said, 'I'm going to Florida State.'"

The "legendary Silver Slipper," a part of Tallahassee's dining and entertainment landscape since 1938, is owned by the Kalfas family. Chris Kalfas played on FSU's first football team in 1947. A unique feature is the Wall of Fame with pictures of celebrities who have dined there, including Coach Pete.

PETE'S SUCCESS STORY CONTINUES

Coaching Success begins with Coach Peterson

Assistant Coaches who went on to become Head Coaches

Coach	Team(s) Coached
John Coatta	Wisconsin ('67-'69), Minnesota State ('70-'75)
Vince Gibson	Kansas State ('67-'74), Louisville ('75-'79), Tulane ('80-'82)
Don James	Washington ('74-'92); Kent State ('71-'73)
Ken Meyer	San Francisco 49ers (1977)
Bobby Bowden	Samford, ('59-'62), West Virginia ('70-'75), Florida State ('76-'09)
Gene McDowell	UCF ('85-'97)
Joe Gibbs	Redskins ('81-'92,'04-'08)
Dan Henning	Falcons ('83-'86); Chargers ('89-'91)
Al Conover	Rice ('72-'75)
Y. C. McNease	Idaho ('68-'69)

Pete's Assistants who became NFL assistant coaches

Don Breaux	NFL assistant for the Oilers, Redskins and Jets
Bobby Jackson	NFL assistant for Falcons, Chargers, Cardinals, Redskins, Rams, Dolphins.

Coach Peterson's Pipeline to the Pros

Quarterback Gary Huff, who signed an NFL contract with the Chicago Bears and later worked in finance with the Oakland Raiders, said: "When I went into Pro ball it took them about five years to catch up with where Coach Peterson had us with the passing game at Florida State, especially with the audibles and route adjustments he had us doing in college."

Consequently, Peterson developed a pipeline to the Pros for Florida State players that is still beneficial to the Seminoles of today! Peterson had 43 players go on to the NFL or AFL before the leagues combined. Twenty-two of the current NFL teams drafted Pete's players between 1961-1973.

The San Diego Chargers lead the group of teams who signed Peterson players with seven, followed by the Oakland Raiders who signed five and the Miami Dolphins with four.

Peterson's high-powered passing attack received great interest among the professionals with 13 receivers (seven TEs and six WRs) being selected. Five quarterbacks were picked by the Pros as well as nine offensive linemen.

Bill Peterson's Pro Players Drafted & Free Agents

1961: Tony Romeo (TE) Washington Redskins

1962: Don Donatelli (C) St. Louis Cardinals
       Ed Trancygier (QB) Washington Redskins

1963: Keith Kinderman (RB) San Diego Chargers (AFL); Green Bay
Packers   (NFL)

1964: Bill Dawson (TE) Los Angeles Rams (NFL); Boston Patriots (AFL)

1965: Fred Biletnikoff (FL) Oakland Raiders (AFL); Detroit Lions (NFL)
       Steve Tensi (QB) San Diego Chargers (AFL); Baltimore Colts (NFL)
       Don Floyd (E) San Diego Chargers (AFL)
       Jack Edwards (C) San Diego Chargers (AFL)
       Frank Pennie (OT) Oakland Raiders (AFL)
       Dick Hermann (LB) Oakland Raiders (AFL)

1966: Jack Shinholser (LB) Washington Redskins (NFL); Oakland Raiders
          (AFL)
       Jim Mankins (FB) Green Bay Packers (NFL); Miami Dolphins (AFL)
       Bill McDowell (LB) San Diego Chargers (AFL)
       Joe Avezanno (C) Boston Patriots (AFL)
       Max Wettstein (TE) Denver Broncos

1967: Del Williams (C) New Orleans Saints
       Larry Kissam (T) Miami Dolphins
       Les Murdock (K) New York Giants

1968: Kim Hammond (QB) Miami Dolphins
       Lane Fenner (FL) San Diego Chargers
       Thurston Taylor (TE) Philadelphia Eagles
       Bill Moremen (RB) New York Giants
       Wayne McDuffie (C) Cleveland Browns

> Dick Hermann (#66)

118

1969:   Ron Sellers (SE) Boston Patriots
        Chip Glass (TE) Cleveland Browns
        Bill Rhodes (G) St. Louis Cardinals
        Walt Sumner (DB) Cleveland Browns
        Dale McCullers (LB) Miami Dolphins

1970:   Bill Cappleman (QB) Minnesota Vikings
        Grant Guthrie (K) Buffalo Bills
        Jeff Churchin (OT) Chicago Bears
        Phil Abraira (DB) Chicago Bears

1971:   Tom Bailey (RB) Philadelphia Eagles

Kim Hammond (#11)

1972:   Rhett Dawson (WR) Houston Oilers
        Richard Amman (DE) Dallas Cowboys
        Kent Gaydos (TE) Oakland Raiders

1973:   Barry Smith (WR) Green Bay Packers
        J. T. Thomas (DB) Pittsburgh Steelers
        Gary Huff (QB) Chicago Bears
        Eddie McMillen (DB) Los Angeles Rams
        Charlie Hunt (LB) San Francisco 49ers
        Gary Parris (TE) San Diego Chargers

**Gary Huff (Bears) was one of five Peterson
QBs drafted by the NFL. Others were:**
Steve Tensi (Chargers)
Ed Trancygier (Redskins)
Kim Hammond (Patriots)
Bill Cappleman (Vikings)

Breakdown of NFL Teams Picking Pete's Players

NFL Team	# Taken
San Diego Chargers	7
Oakland Raiders	5
Miami Dolphins	4
Chicago Bears	3
Green Bay Packers	3
New England Patriots	3
Washington Redskins	3
Denver Broncos	2
New York Giants	2
Philadelphia Eagles	2
Cleveland Browns	2
Los Angeles Rams	2
St. Louis Cardinals	2
Detroit Lions	1
Baltimore Colts	1
New Orleans Saints	1
Minnesota Vikings	1
Buffalo Bills	1
Houston Oilers	1
Dallas Cowboys	1
Pittsburgh Steelers	1
San Francisco 49ers	1

*Total exceeds individual number of Pete's Players selected because some were chosen by teams from both leagues before the NFL and AFL combined.

Honors and Awards-Peterson Era

Hall of Fame

Bill Peterson- Florida Sports Hall of Fame
Fred Biletnikoff- College Football Hall of Fame; NFL Pro Football Hall of Fame
Ron Sellers-College Football Hall of Fame
Bobby Bowden-College Football Hall of Fame

Consensus All Americans

Fred Biletnikoff
Ron Sellers

All Americans

Gene McDowell ('62)
Fred Biletnikoff ('64)
Jack Shinholser   ('65)
Gary Pajcic ('66)
Del Williams ('66)
Kim Hammond ('67)
Ron Sellers ('67,'68)
Dale McCullers ('68)
Jack Fenwick ('68)
Bill Cappleman '68)
Rhett Dawson ('71)
Gary Huff ('71)
J. T. Thomas ('71)

Academic All-American

Gary Huff ('72)

All South Independent First Team

16 players ('68-'70)

Florida State University Hall of Fame

23 players

NFL Super Bowl Participants

Dale McCullers- Colts-1969
Ron Sellers-Dolphins '73
Fred Biletnikoff-Raiders '68 & '77
J. T. Thomas-Steelers- 1975, '76, '79

One final thought from Bill Peterson:

"THIS IS THE GREATEST COUNTRY IN AMERICA!"

One of Peterson's marquee wins inspired this sign
outside of a Tallahassee hotel.

"PETE'S POSTS"

"Coach Pete" strode the Seminole's sidelines as Head Football Coach from 1960 through 1970. Though FSU's very young football tradition was already strong, Bill Peterson's visionary leadership and offensive genius introduced the Seminoles to a national audience, and revolutionized college football in the south.

Peterson was the first to apply a pro-style passing attack to the college game, and his schemes produced many of the great stars of that era, including All-American linebacker Gene McDowell, receivers Fred Biletnikoff (All-American, Pro Hall of Fame) and Ron Sellers (All-American, College Hall of Fame). The progressive-minded Peterson also recruited the first African-American to play for FSU, All-American defensive back J.T. Thomas. With his great leadership abilities, Peterson was the first to lead the Seminoles to a victory over the Florida Gators.

Peterson was especially renown for surrounding himself with great football minds whose later careers reflected his eye for excellence. Bobby Bowden, Don James, Dan Henning, Bill Parcells, Vince Gibson, John Coatta, Al Conover, Ken Meyer, and Joe Gibbs are just a few of the famous names who served at FSU as assistants to the legendary Bill Peterson.

Bill Peterson's teams always entered the field running between the twin supports of the old "H" shaped goal posts, common to that era. In tribute to Coach Pete, to his players & coaches, The Peterson Family has made possible the re-installation of the historic "H" goal posts in storied Doak Campbell Stadium. These will forever be known as "Pete's Posts."

Florida State's Lasting Tribute
to Coach Bill Peterson

"Pete's Posts" on Bobby Bowden Field at Doak Campbell Stadium – the football stadium of Florida State University.